All The Jazz CHORDS You'll Ever Need!

ISBN 978-0-7119-7769-3

Compiled by Jack Long
Cover design by Chloë Alexander

Visit Hal Leonard Online at
www.halleonard.com

World headquarters, contact:
Hal Leonard
7777 West Bluemound Road
Milwaukee, WI 53213
Email: info@halleonard.com

In Europe, contact:
Hal Leonard Europe Limited
1 Red Place
London, W1K 6PL
Email: info@halleonardeurope.com

In Australia, contact:
Hal Leonard Australia Pty. Ltd.
4 Lentara Court
Cheltenham, Victoria, 3192 Australia
Email: info@halleonard.com.au

Introductory Notes

1 The chords in this book are voiced in a way that makes them easy to find and play effectively. But that doesn't mean you can't play them differently if you want to.

The notes contained in the right hand can be rearranged in any order you like, and will still represent the chord symbol shown, like this:

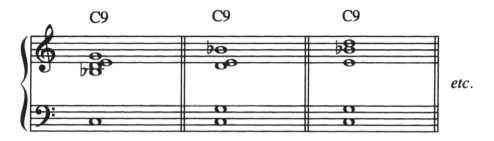

etc.

The left hand can also be changed to alter the chord structure. Sometimes, when this is specifically required, the left hand alteration will be indicated by a 'cut' (or 'slash') chord, consisting of a chord symbol followed by a sloping line (the 'cut' or 'slash'), followed by the root, or bass note, that you need to play. C/E, for instance, means that a chord of C is to be played with an E root, or bass note.

Here's one way of playing that:

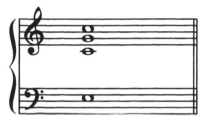

In addition, you will often see 'cut' chords containing a root not found in the chord itself. Am7/D, for instance, played like this...

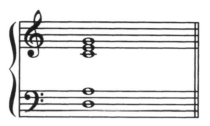

... is actually D11, described in a more commonly understood fashion for those who may not know what D11 means. Now, however, with the help of this book, you will never have any trouble playing D11 - or, indeed, any other chords you are likely to be faced with!

2 The following keys are not covered here: C♯, D♯, F♯, G♯ and A♯. They are identical to, respectively, D♭, E♭, G♭, A♭ and B♭ (which *are* covered) and are played exactly the same.

3 Some keys (C, E♭, E, F, A and B♭) contain more chords than the others. If you come across these additional chords in any of the keys which *don't* have them, you will be able to work them out easily from the nearest example (e.g., the notes in a G chord are two semitones up from those in F).

C Chords

C major - C

C suspended 4th - Csus or Csus4

C augmented 5th - C+ or Caug

C added 6th - C6

C added 6th and 9th - C6/9

C major 7th - Cmaj7

C Chords

C dominant 7th - C7

C dominant 7th with suspended 4th - C7sus or C7sus4

C dominant 7th with flattened 5th - C7(♭5)

C dominant 7th with augmented 5th - C7+ or C7aug

C dominant 7th with flattened 9th - C7(♭9)

C dominant 7th with sharpened 9th - C7(♯9)

C major 9th - Cmaj9

C dominant 9th - C9

C dominant 9th with sharpened 11th - C9(#11)
with flattened 5th - C9(b5)

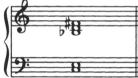

C dominant 11th - C11

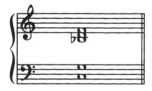

C dominant 13th - C13

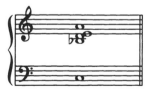

C minor - Cm

C Chords

C diminished - C° or Cdim

C minor added 6th - Cm6

C minor 7th - Cm7

C minor 7th with flattened 5th - Cm7(♭5)

C minor added major 7th - Cm(maj7)

C minor 9th - Cm9

D♭ Chords

D♭ major - D♭

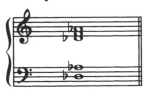

D♭ suspended 4th - D♭sus or D♭sus4

D♭ augmented 5th - D♭+ or D♭aug

D♭ added 6th - D♭6

D♭ added 6th and 9th - D♭6/9

D♭ major 7th - D♭maj7

D♭ Chords

D♭ dominant 7th - D♭7

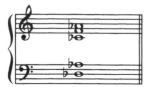

D♭ dominant 7th with flattened 9th - D♭7(♭9)

D♭ dominant 7th with sharpened 9th - D♭7(♯9)

D♭ dominant 9th - D♭9

D♭ dominant 11th - D♭11

D♭ dominant 13th - D♭13

Db minor - Dbm

Db diminished - Db° or Dbdim

Db minor added 6th - Dbm6

Db minor 7th - Dbm7

Db minor 7th with flattened 5th - Dbm7(b5)

Db minor 9th - Dbm9

D Chords

D major - D

D suspended 4th - Dsus or Dsus4

D augmented 5th - D+ or Daug

D added 6th - D6

D added 6th and 9th - D6/9

D major 7th - Dmaj7

D dominant 7th - D7

D dominant 7th with flattened 9th - D7(♭9)

D dominant 7th with sharpened 9th - D7(♯9)

D dominant 9th - D9

D dominant 11th - D11

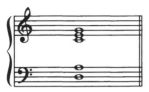

D dominant 13th - D13

D Chords

D minor - Dm

D diminished - D° or Ddim

D minor added 6th - Dm6

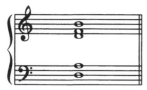

D minor 7th - Dm7

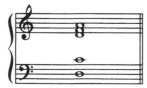

D minor 7th with flattened 5th - Dm7(♭5)

D minor 9th - Dm9

E♭ Chords

Eb major - Eb

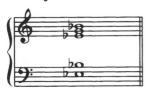 

Eb suspended 4th - Ebsus or Ebsus4

Eb augmented 5th - Eb+ or Ebaug

Eb added 6th - Eb6

Eb added 6th and 9th - Eb6/9

Eb major 7th - Ebmaj7

E♭ Chords

E♭ dominant 7th - E♭7

E♭ dominant 7th with suspended 4th - E♭7sus or E♭7sus4

E♭ dominant 7th with flattened 5th - E♭7(♭5)

E♭ dominant 7th with augmented 5th - E♭7+ or E♭7aug

E♭ dominant 7th with flattened 9th - E♭7(♭9)

E♭ dominant 7th with sharpened 9th - E♭7(♯9)

E♭ major 9th - E♭maj9

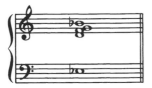

E♭ dominant 9th - E♭9

E♭ dominant 9th with sharpened 11th - E♭9(♯11)
with flattened 5th - E♭9(♭5)

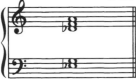

E♭ dominant 11th - E♭11

E♭ dominant 13th - E♭13

E♭ minor - E♭m

E♭ Chords

E♭ diminished - E♭° or E♭dim

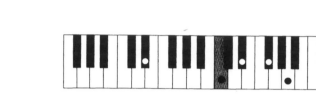

E♭ minor added 6th - E♭m6

E♭ minor 7th - E♭m7

E♭ minor 7th with flattened 5th - E♭m7(♭5)

E♭ minor added major 7th - E♭m(maj7)

E♭ minor 9th - E♭m9

E Chords

E major - E

E suspended 4th - Esus or Esus4

E augmented 5th - E+ or Eaug

E added 6th - E6

E added 6th and 9th - E6/9

E major 7th - Emaj7

E Chords

E dominant 7th - E7

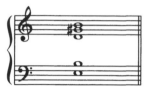 

E dominant 7th with suspended 4th - E7sus or E7sus4

E dominant 7th with flattened 5th - E7(♭5)

E dominant 7th with augmented 5th - E7+ or E7aug

E dominant 7th with flattened 9th - E7(♭9)

E dominant 7th with sharpened 9th - E7(♯9)

E major 9th - Emaj9

E dominant 9th - E9

E dominant 9th with sharpened 11th - E9(♯11)
with flattened 5th - E9(♭5)

E dominant 11th - E11

E dominant 13th - E13

E minor - Em

E Chords

E diminished - E° or Edim

E minor added 6th - Em6

E minor 7th - Em7

E minor 7th with flattened 5th - Em7(♭5)

E minor added major 7th - Em(maj7)

E minor 9th - Em9

F Chords

F major - F

F suspended 4th - Fsus or Fsus4

F augmented 5th - F+ or Faug

F added 6th - F6

F added 6th and 9th - F6/9

F major 7th - Fmaj7

F Chords

F dominant 7th - F7

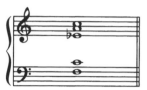 

F dominant 7th with suspended 4th - F7sus or F7sus4

F dominant 7th with flattened 5th - F7(♭5)

F dominant 7th with augmented 5th - F7+ or F7aug

F dominant 7th with flattened 9th - F7(♭9)

F dominant 7th with sharpened 9th - F7(♯9)

F major 9th - Fmaj9

F dominant 9th - F9

F dominant 9th with sharpened 11th - F9(#11)
with flattened 5th - F9(♭5)

F dominant 11th - F11

F dominant 13th - F13

F minor - Fm

F Chords

F diminished - F° or Fdim

F minor added 6th - Fm6

F minor 7th - Fm7

F minor 7th with flattened 5th - Fm7(♭5)

F minor added major 7th - Fm(maj7)

F minor 9th - Fm9

G♭ Chords

G♭ major - G♭

G♭ suspended 4th - G♭sus or G♭sus4

G♭ augmented 5th - G♭+ or G♭aug

G♭ added 6th - G♭6

G♭ added 6th and 9th - G♭6/9

G♭ major 7th - G♭maj7

G♭ Chords

G♭ dominant 7th - G♭7

G♭ dominant 7th with flattened 9th - G♭7(♭9)

G♭ dominant 7th with sharpened 9th - G♭7(♯9)

G♭ dominant 9th - G♭9

G♭ dominant 11th - G♭11

G♭ dominant 13th - G♭13

G♭ minor - G♭m

G♭ diminished - G♭° or G♭dim

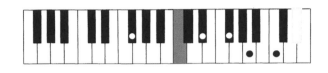

G♭ minor added 6th - G♭m6

G♭ minor 7th - G♭m7

G♭ minor 7th with flattened 5th - G♭m7(♭5)

G♭ minor 9th - G♭m9

G Chords

G major - G

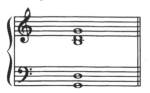

G suspended 4th - Gsus or Gsus4

G augmented 5th - G+ or Gaug

G added 6th - G6

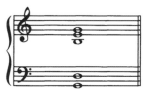

G added 6th and 9th - G6/9

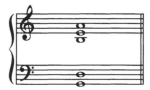

G major 7th - Gmaj7

G dominant 7th - G7

G dominant 7th with flattened 9th - G7(♭9)

G dominant 7th with sharpened 9th - G7(♯9)

G dominant 9th - G9

G dominant 11th - G11

G dominant 13th - G13

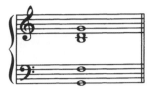

G Chords

G minor - Gm

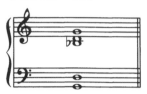

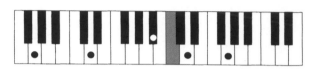

G diminished - G° or Gdim

G minor added 6th - Gm6

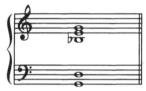

G minor 7th - Gm7

G minor 7th with flattened 5th - Gm7(♭5)

G minor 9th - Gm9

A♭ Chords

Ab major - Ab

Ab suspended 4th - Absus or Absus4

Ab augmented 5th - Ab+ or Abaug

Ab added 6th - Ab6

Ab added 6th and 9th - Ab6/9

Ab major 7th - Abmaj7

A♭ Chords

A♭ dominant 7th - A♭7

A♭ dominant 7th with flattened 9th - A♭7(♭9)

A♭ dominant 7th with sharpened 9th - A♭7(♯9)

A♭ dominant 9th - A♭9

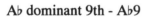 

A♭ dominant 11th - A♭11

A♭ dominant 13th - A♭13

A♭ minor - A♭m

A♭ diminished - A♭° or A♭dim

A♭ minor added 6th - A♭m6

A♭ minor 7th - A♭m7

A♭ minor 7th with flattened 5th - A♭m7(♭5)

A♭ minor 9th - A♭m9

A Chords

A major - A

A suspended 4th - Asus or Asus4

A augmented 5th - A+ or Aaug

A added 6th - A6

A added 6th and 9th - A6/9

A major 7th - Amaj7

A dominant 7th - A7

A dominant 7th with suspended 4th - A7sus or A7sus4

A dominant 7th with flattened 5th - A7(♭5)

A dominant 7th with augmented 5th - A7+ or A7aug

A dominant 7th with flattened 9th - A7(♭9)

A dominant 7th with sharpened 9th - A7(♯9)

A Chords

A major 9th - Amaj9

A dominant 9th - A9

A dominant 9th with sharpened 11th - A9(#11)
with flattened 5th - A9(♭5)

A dominant 11th - A11

A dominant 13th - A13

A minor - Am

A diminished - A° or Adim

A minor added 6th - Am6

A minor 7th - Am7

A minor 7th with flattened 5th - Am7(♭5)

A minor added major 7th - Am(maj7)

A minor 9th - Am9

B♭ Chords

B♭ major - B♭

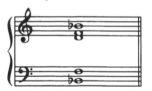

B♭ suspended 4th - B♭sus or B♭sus4

B♭ augmented 5th - B♭+ or B♭aug

B♭ added 6th - B♭6

B♭ added 6th and 9th - B♭6/9

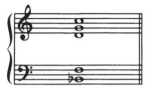

B♭ major 7th - B♭maj7

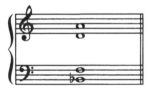

B♭ dominant 7th - B♭7

B♭ dominant 7th with suspended 4th - B♭7sus or B♭7sus4

B♭ dominant 7th with flattened 5th - B♭7(♭5)

B♭ dominant 7th with augmented 5th - B♭7+ or B♭7aug

B♭ dominant 7th with flattened 9th - B♭7(♭9)

B♭ dominant 7th with sharpened 9th - B♭7(♯9)

B♭ Chords

B♭ major 9th - B♭maj9

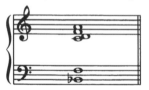

B♭ dominant 9th - B♭9

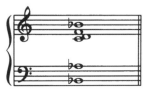

B♭ dominant 9th with sharpened 11th - B♭9(#11)
with flattened 5th - B♭9(♭5)

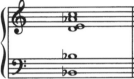

B♭ dominant 11th - B♭11

B♭ dominant 13th - B♭13

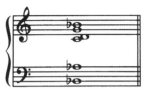

B♭ minor - B♭m

Bb diminished - Bb° or Bbdim

Bb minor added 6th - Bbm6

Bb minor 7th - Bbm7

Bb minor 7th with flattened 5th - Bbm7(b5)

Bb minor added major 7th - Bbm(maj7)

Bb minor 9th - Bbm9

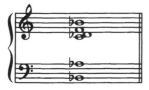

B Chords

B major - B

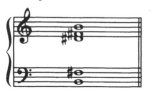

B suspended 4th - Bsus or Bsus4

B augmented 5th - B+ or Baug

B added 6th - B6

B added 6th and 9th - B6/9

B major 7th - Bmaj7

B dominant 7th - B7

B dominant 7th with flattened 9th - B7(♭9)

B dominant 7th with sharpened 9th - B7(#9)

B dominant 9th - B9

B dominant 11th - B11

B dominant 13th - B13

B Chords

B minor - Bm

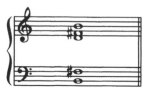

B diminished - B° or Bdim

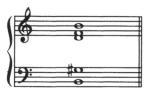

B minor added 6th - Bm6

B minor 7th - Bm7

B minor 7th with flattened 5th - Bm7(♭5)

B minor 9th - Bm9

Index